It Seems That I'm Depressed

疑似抑郁症

It Seems That I'm Depressed

疑似抑郁症

Man Chen 漫尘

translated by

Ouyang Yu 欧阳昱

PUNCHER & WATTMANN

First published in 2021
Published by Puncher and Wattmann
PO Box 279
Waratah NSW 2298

http://www.puncherandwattmann.com
puncherandwattmann@bigpond.com

NATIONAL
LIBRARY
OF AUSTRALIA

A catalogue entry for this book is available from the National Library of Australia.

ISBN   9781925780642

Cover design by Miranda Douglas
Printed by Lightning Source International

Contents

在闪电下面	8	Under the Lightning
果壳嵌进我的肉里	10	The Fruit Shell Stuck in My Flesh
我看着我做梦	12	I Watched Myself Dreaming
地下室听雨	14	Listening to the Rain in the Basement
俯冲	16	Diving
体味	18	Body Odour
短发女孩	20	The Girl with Short Hair
禅坐	22	Sitting Meditation
斋戒	24	Fasting
天，就要暗下来了	26	The Sky, About to Darken
寨子	28	In the Stockade Village
春风紧	30	Spring Wind Close
大片	32	A Blockbuster
沉默	34	Silence
泥瓦工	36	The Mason
发胀	38	Swelling Up
昨夜九点四十	40	At 9.40 Last Night
感应	42	Telepathy
夜风四起	44	The Night Wind Rose in All Directions
江湖	46	Rivers and Lakes
风暴	48	The Storm
悼亡灵	50	Mourning the Dead Souls
有一种欢聚	52	A Happy Getting-Together
大山里的春色	54	Colours of the Spring in the Mountains
我索性被绿色包围	56	I Simply Let Myself Be Surrounded with the Colour Green
祭酒	58	Libation
我为什么喜欢酒	60	Why Do I Love Liquor?

三人行	62	Three of Them, Walking Together
祂们	64	Them
谍战	66	The Espionage War
诗 / 大卡	68	Poetry/Truck
新生物	70	Things That Are New
湿天出行	72	Going Out on a Wet Day
演化	74	Evolution
水樱桃	76	Water Cherries
催眠	78	Hypnosis
易拉罐	80	Pop-Up Cans
尖叫	82	Screaming
疑似抑郁症	84	It Seems That I'm Depressed
跑题	86	A Digression
美少女日记	88	Diary Entry, by a Beautiful Girl
海拉尔	90	Hai—La—Erh
数数	92	Counting the Numbers
"闯虎穴"	94	'Storming into a Tiger's Den'
好的，瑞雪	96	Alright, Auspicious Snow
求救腔	98	Sounding the Alarm
心脏搭桥者言	100	Thus Spoke the One Having Gone Through the Heart Bypass
江小白	102	River Little White (Or Jiang Xiao Bai)
金色烟蒂	106	A Golden Butt
暴雨核心	108	The Centre of the Storm

在闪电下面

当夏夜被闪电擦亮
勾勒出世界的峥嵘面目
就有人戴着铁链在空中行走

空气潮湿，想稀释一朵花的恐惧
也想找一根金属，将自然的喧哗与骚动
收回大地

我猜想，此时有许多人在匆忙奔走
低头，噤声，躲避从前犯下的罪错
可有的人一去不回，惊落蜡白的脸

我的心也迸出一道闪电
在沉闷的体内
穿刺一下

Under the Lightning

When the summer night was lit by lightning
delineating the fierce features of the world
someone was walking in the air, in chains

the air moist, intending to dilute the fears of a flower
and to find back a piece of metal, retrieving to the earth
nature's sound and fury

I was guessing that, right now, many might have been hurrying
heads lowered, voices withheld, to avoid the crime committed before
but there were some who had left without return, their candle-pale faces dropped

a lightning that also leapt out of my heart
jabbing
inside my boring body

果壳嵌进我的肉里

坚硬果壳来自热带
绛紫色表面光滑似铁
吸收了阳光，月露，泥土气
经过同类引导，竟成了凶器

不存心较量，也不是任意宰割
彼此心怀敌意，又相互寻找缺口
在我用力掰开它的时候，果壳深深嵌进
我的肉里，疼痛一轮轮袭来

它要长进我身体，享受我的呻吟
让我以后的日子羞于后悔
且痛定思痛：既然是异类
何不各安其所，各流其血

The Fruit Shell Stuck in My Flesh

The hard fruit shell was from the tropics
and its dark reddish purple surface was as smooth as iron
having absorbed the sun, the moon's dew and the smell of the earth
it, guided by its fellow shells, turned into a lethal weapon

not intending to take me on or to cut me at will
it and I were mutually hostile, while looking for each other's loopholes
as I applied full force in prying it open, the shell made a deep cut
in my flesh as round after round of pain attacked me

it would grow into my body and enjoy my moans
making my days ashamed of regrets
and dwell in pain: since we are alien to each other
why don't we shed our own separate blood, at ease in our separate abode?

我看着我做梦

一缕轻烟的我，看着我沉下去
触冰山一角。海水冰凉
灌进我意识的每一间仓房
沉下去，如婴儿抱黑铁
看我进入真实的虚构
几千只红嘴雀一言不发
拖一位黑衣人在壁龛前
忏悔

床，滋长爱与恨的温床
开满玫瑰和罂粟的五尺之亩
我大大张开，也蜷缩如蝉蛹
上一季拌醅发酵的自酿酒
一阵阵，制造血液潮汐
而黑衣人，站在千米堤坝
纵身一跃

我看见，我从水中升起来
眼睑像菩提叶
昼夜不分地掀动

I Watched Myself Dreaming

I, a wisp of smoke, watched myself sink
hitting the tip of the iceberg. The seawater was icy cold
filling each and every warehouse of my consciousness
sinking, like a baby hugging black iron
watching myself enter into real fiction
while thousands of red-mouthed birds remained silent
dragging a black-clothed man to confessions
at the shrine

the bed, the hotbed that bred love and hatred
was a five-foot mu of overgrown roses and poppies*
where I lay wide open as I curled up like a chrysalis
the wine, self-made and fermenting, last season
was creating wave after tidal wave of blood
while the black-clothed man jumped off
the thousand-meter-long embankment

I saw myself rise in water
my eyelids like the pipal-tree leaves
batting day and night

---

*   Translator's note: One mu is a unit of area equivalent to 0.0667 hectares.

地下室听雨

没错，这就是砸，噼啪噼啪噼噼啪啪
把伪灯火砸晕
把男人砸成多肉植物
砸成行动侏儒
女人砸成追自己尾巴玩的猫咪
翻过一道道
草栅栏

再砸下去，世界从花脸
砸成铜头黑脸
没错，单皮鼓敲得正紧
咚锵咚锵咚锵咚锵咚咚咚咚
采采采采，哐采哐采哐
"蓝脸的多尔敦盗御马"

我在地下室边听边摸
摸一颗未受潮的炸弹
地面上的那些
关我鸟事

Listening to the Rain in the Basement

Make no mistake for that's smashing, with bang bang bang bang bang
Till false lightings felt dizzy
And men became fleshy plants
Midgets in action
While women were turned into my baby cats that chased their own tails
Climbing over one after another
Grassy fence

If the smashing went on, the world would be turned from a flowery face
Into a bronze head and black face
Whomp whomp whomp whomp whomp whomp whomp
Ba-donk-a-donk, ba-donk-a-donk, ba-donk-a-donk
'The blue-faced Dolton has stolen the royal horse'

As I listened in the basement, I touched
A bomb, not yet moistened
All those others above ground
Had fuck all to do with me

俯冲

没有预演，只要高兴
我就收起翅膀
从几十米空中直坠而下
气流震动
我无法描述血冲大脑时的
颠顶与豪壮
只要高兴，我可以地面开花

可那是平静水面
我看见水里的另一个我
正对准自己猛撞过来
这多么虚幻多么真实
面对面的毁灭是多么无趣
一瞬间，我重又弹开双翅
在天水间完成一个 V

Diving

No rehearsals, as long as I am happy
I'll fold my wings
And plunge straight from scores of meters on high
Airflows vibrating
I can't describe the muddle-headedness and glory
When blood rushed to my brain
As long as I am happy, I can burst into bloom on the ground

But that's the placid water
Where I can see another me in it
Plunging right into me
So illusory and real
Destruction, face to face, is so boring
In an instant, I flip open my wings
Completing a V, between the water and the skies

体味

等级考第 N 试场
新疆班的考生如期而来
他们卷发，短髭
隆鼻，坳眼
黝亮的皮肤散发出
孜然、牛羊和青草的
气息

这种气息在第二场考试
就消失了
取而代之的是
自来水中的氯气味
那些汉族的考生
真的有些寡淡

而每次与西班牙外教
Leesa 擦肩而过
CHANEL 的味道
让人怦然心跳
就像一阵花腔女高音
撩你耳蜗

Body Odour

In the No. N examination room, for a grade examination
The examinees from Xinjiang arrived as expected
Curly hair, short moustaches
High noses, sunken eyes
Their shiny skins sending forth
A smell
Of cumin, cows and sheep
And green grass

This smell had disappeared
In the second examination
Replaced by
That of chlorine in the tap water
The Han-Chinese examinees
Were really vapid

And every time when I go past Leesa
A Spanish teacher
The Chanel on her
Causes my heart to give a leap
Like a coloratura soprano
That tickles your cochlea

短发女孩

沉默。黑眼睑。银色鼻环。
纹身。蓝蝴蝶。短皮鞭。蓝璎珞。
黑色体恤。半开半合的嘴唇。
胸。两座山岗。起伏的嘴唇。
肚脐。小漩涡。小腹。半张蝴蝶翅膀。
膝盖。牛仔洞。渔网。网。大腿网。
沉默。膝盖。大头鞋。鞋钉。
沉默。冷气眸子。头盔。摩托。
斜支架。口香糖。紫葡萄嘴唇。
车站。人流。行李箱。轮子。沉默河流。
短发。碎刘海。不对称。内扣。
红蓝相间。闪电。短发。城市。流莺。
玻璃窗户。父母。眼睛。渐入。渐出。

The Girl with Short Hair

Silent. Black eyelids. A silver nose-ring.

Tattooed. Blue butterfly. A short leather cloak. A blue necklace.

A black T-shirt. Half-opened lips.

Breasts. Two hills. Heaving lips.

The navel. A tiny whorl. Half-opened butterfly wings.

The knees. Holes in the jeans. Fishnet. Net. Thigh-net.

Silent. Knees. Big-toed shoes. Hobnails.

Silent. Cold pupils. Helmet. Motorcycle.

Diagonal bracket. Gum. Purple grape lips.

Train station. Crowd. Suitcase. Wheels. A silent river.

Short hair. A fragmentary fringe. Nonsymmetrical. Buttons underneath.

Blue over red. Flash of lightning. Short hair. City. A flowing oriole.*

Glazed windows. Parents. Eyes. Fade in. Fade out.

---

*   Translator's note: A euphemism for a prostitute.

禅坐

双足跏趺
脊直肩张
手结定印于脐下
头中正
双眼微闭
舌舐上腭
面带微笑

广宁寺的来了方丈
向俗家女弟子
传授禅坐心法
他用中指和食指
捏起女弟子的
脚踝

轻放在线条圆润的

Sitting Meditation

Cross-legged
Straight-backed
Hands, in a knot, placed underneath the navel
Head held straight up
Eyes slightly closed
The tip of the tongue against the roof of the mouth
A smile on the face

The Buddhist abbot has arrived at Guangning Temple
Teaching the lay female disciples
How to sit in meditation
With his middle finger and index finger
He picks up the ankle of one disciple

Gently putting it at the root
Of his thighs where the lines are round and mellow

斋戒

啖肉，喝酒，肉身沉坠
灵魂带血的嘶喊

驱赶体内的戾兽
——在月圆涨潮之夜

兽爪的肉垫贴近你的情穴
欲望是一张天堂门票

压在烛台底下
摘几颗曼陀罗和无花果

从容地碾碎
所有的罪孽如豆腐

寡淡而柔软
你的目光是一片菜园

篱墙外，一只饥饿的绵羊对着青草
下跪

Fasting

I eat meat, I drink, my body sinking
My soul shrieking with blood

To drive the violent animal inside my body
—on a night of a round moon and a rising tide

The fleshy pads of the animal claws are close to the hole of your love
Desire is but an admission ticket to heavens

Pick a few mandala and figs
And put them under the candlestick

Grind all the sins at ease
To pieces like tofu

Vapid and soft
Your eyes are the spread of a vegetable garden

Outside the fence, a hungry sheep is kneeling
In front of the green grass

天，就要暗下来了

上天绷了一天的脸，累了
从无名指上褪下金戒指
在云头撒最后一网
小鹬子拼命扑翅膀
它的渺小逃不出我眼睛

天，真的就要暗下来
光线收回了剩余的热情
池塘一点点缩小
小到记忆的核
可我看得清楚，再小
它的娇润仍留在体内

天渐渐暗下来
像灰色的液体慢慢注入血液
这其实伤害不到任何人
只要我心中能燃起火苗
夜色就永远合不拢
反倒成了无边的怀抱

The Sky, About to Darken

The face of the sky, tightened all day, had grown weary
As it took off the gold ring from its ring finger
And cast the last net on the head of a cloud
A little sparrow hawk, its wings fluttering, was trying its hardest
Its littleness unable to escape from my eyes

The sky was really about to darken
Lights were retrieving the remaining passion
The pond was getting smaller, bit by bit
Till it became the core of memory
But I could clearly see that its delicacy still remained
In its body however small it was

The sky was darkening now
Injecting into the blood, like a grey liquid
Which, in fact, didn't hurt anyone
As long as tongues of flame could flare up in my heart
The colours of the night wouldn't close
On the contrary, they would turn into a boundless embrace

寨子

一棵树引来一条路
蚂蚁跑得欢
遇到了栅栏，或是石砌围墙
就分头行动。这群皂衣小贼
想包围一座古老的寨子

三角梅在墙头放哨
风中的石头和水中的石头立场坚定
共同守卫一口井，两座谷仓，三道畜栏
五六层梯田
甚至一片绿叶就是一名卫士
听从长老的命令，掩护妇女和儿童

可是路上偏偏走来了一位异乡女子
一双鹭鸶长脚轻盈而好奇
面对她结婚生子的强烈愿望
清风寨子
自酿酒般摇晃，旋转

因为，那女子的身后
闪烁着另一道迷煞人的风景

In the Stockade Village

A tree led to a road
The ants were running with delight
If they encountered a fence or a stone retaining wall
They'd act in different ways. These little black-clothed thieves
Were intending to surround the ancient village

The bougainvillea stood guard on top of the wall
The stone in the wind and in the water took a firm position
Mutually guarding a well, two barns, three corrals
And five or six terraced fields
Even a green leaf could be a security guard
Who listened to the elder's order and gave cover to kids and women

But, of all the people, a woman from elsewhere was walking on the road
Her long egret legs brisk and curious
In the face of her strong desire to get married and have kids
This village of clean wind
Started shaking and turning, as if drunken on its own brewed wine

Because behind the woman
Was flashing another landscape, so killingly attractive

春风紧

被释放的生命，脱离衣裤
在晾衣绳上翻飞
远处的桃花，在原定区域
与以往一样开始喘息，作嗲

而春风似乎更加留恋澡堂和
厨房，让头发和蔬菜竞相喷香
轻盈啊，不仅属于被遗弃的事物

我的脚步和土地接受云的邀请
享受阳光美酒，哼一首嫩绿小曲
"开花，不要怀疑灵魂的芳香
今朝的欢乐会成为永久的堡垒……"

那些曾经囤积的幽火
赶紧，找心灵的枝头，绽放
不，凛冽地，复活

Spring Wind Close

Lives, set free, from the clothes and trousers
Were flying over the clothesline
The peach flowers in a distance, in their designated place
Began panting, and behaving in a spoiled manner, like before

And the spring wind seemed to be reluctant to leave the bathroom
And the kitchen, keeping the hair and the vegetables vying in fragrance
Lissomness didn't just belong to things abandoned

My footsteps and the land beneath, invited by the cloud
Enjoyed the sun and wine, humming a tender, green tune
'Let the flowers open and don't doubt the scent of souls
For pleasure today will become an eternal castle...'

The dim fires, stored up
Are hurrying, to find the branches, of hearts, to burst open
Oh, no, to bitingly come alive again

大片

一位先锋诗人
小说家兼翻译家
近来迷上了手机摄影
对球状物与
溅射形线条
尤感兴趣
混凝土上的裂缝
榉树林中落日及碎光
墙角灯烘托出的檵木剪影
晨露在玻璃上私奔
被他的手机一一翻译成
不带字幕的
大片
唯独给他本人拍照
总是用东西遮脸
书，汤匙，黄鹤楼烟，甚至
一根剔得锃亮的鱼刺
都会成为脸的一部分
好像刻意隐瞒
他是一道
球状闪电

A Blockbuster

An avant-garde poet

Novelist and translator

Has recently become obsessed with photographing with his mobile phone

He's particularly interested in

The shapes of balls

And ejaculatory lines

The cracks in the concrete

The setting sun, and the fragmentary lights, in a forest of beech trees

The silhouette of an elm, set off by a lamp in a corner

The morning dew eloping on the windowpane

All these were translated by his phone

Into a blockbuster without caption

The only exception being that when he took photos of himself

He would cover his own face, with things like

A book, a spoon, a pack of Yellow Crane Tower, even

A fishbone picked clean and shiny

All of which became part of his face

Like a deliberate attempt to conceal

His being

A ball lightning

沉默

你再怎么沉默
像老家具
缩在颓废的角落
或像枪口弹尽
残留的烟
你眼中闪着刺刀寒光
就像零下 40 度的冰面冻结舌头
只张着空洞的嘴
哪怕是刚从树上掉下来
不喊疼的姑娘
递上
一串黑树莓
你沉默
比不过一具尸体

除非人们抬着你
向另一具真正的尸体
大声抗议

Silence

However silent you were
Shrunken in a decadent corner
Like old furniture
Or like the residual smoke
On the mouth of a gun that had run out of the bullets
Your eyes were still flashing the chilling light of the bayonet
Like a frozen tongue on the surface of ice, 40 degrees below zero
Only keeping a hollow mouth open
Even if a girl who had just
Dropped out of a tree and didn't complain about the pain
Offered
You a string of black raspberries
You kept silent
Not as silent as a corpse, though

Unless people carried you
In loud protest
Against another real corpse

泥瓦工

皮肤黝亮
小腱子肉
像抹了桐油的榆木疙瘩
翻浆，抄浆，坯浆
托线，吊锤，刮浆
汗珠子掉入草丛冒
烟

午后两点
一堵毛墙的影子
散发出大蒜、干辣椒
和隔夜的苦荞酒味
他们绿胆枯肠
大便干燥
小便酱黄

那个稍显白嫩的年轻人
接过师傅手中的矿泉水
灌满一嘴
"噗——"地，喷洒在
混凝土上

The Mason

Shiny skin
Sinewy
Like blocks of elm wood, smeared with tung oil
Frost boiling, pulping, pumping
A supporting line, a hanging hammer, and solutioning
Till drops of sweat fell into the clusters of grass
Smoking

At 2 p.m.
The shadow of a rough wall
Reeking of garlic, dry chili
And last night's wine of tartary buckwheat
They had green galls and withered intestines
Their excrement dry
Their piss soy-sauce yellow

The young man slightly paler and tenderer
Took the mineral water from his master's hand
And filled his mouth with it
Before he spilled it, with a fizz, onto
The concrete ground

发胀

穿过长长的紫藤廊
阳光在藤叶间闪躲

樱桃树枝条疏朗
阳光就倾泻在低处

马齿苋。车前子。蒲公英
麦冬。地菩……这些匍匐植物

散发迷人气息。和水边石头
一起微微发烫。蜘蛛在水上跳

芭蕾。这天鹅绒的舞台，风一吹
毛茸茸或丝滑的感觉

撑得我有些发胀
好像另一个我正在破壳

Swelling Up

Past the long corridor of purple vines
The sunlight was hiding amidst the vines and leaves

The branches of the cherry trees were sparse
Where the sun poured its light onto the lower ground

Purslane. Asiatic plantain seed. Dandelions.
Dwarf lilyturf roots... all these creepers

Smelt of allurement. Slightly heating up
With the waterside stone. The spider was ballet-dancing on the

Water. The stage with velvet, when a wind blew across it
Gave one a feeling of fur or silk

Swelling me up
As if there was another me breaking out of a shell

昨夜九点四十

昨天己亥猪年农历初六
宜：祭祀、捕捉、解除
余事勿取
忌：嫁娶、安葬、不归

历史上这天的重大事件
最早是公元 618 年
隋炀帝死于兵变
隋朝灭亡

而 1400 多年后的一个晚上
九点半才散的酒局
我脚步飘忽，沿华亭湖往西走
竟然听到有青蛙在叫

十分钟后，我看到了手机上
人类第一张黑洞的照片
像一只充血的蛙眼
在银河系中心瞪我回家

At 9.40 Last Night

It was January 6th in the Year of Pigs
Fitting: to hold sacrificial ceremonies, to catch, to free
not to take additional things
Forbidding: to get married, to have funerals, to have no returns

Great events in history on this day
The earliest in A.D. 618
When Emperor Yang of Sui died of a mutiny
And the Sui dynasty came to its demise

And on a night 1400 years subsequently
With a dinner just finished at 9.30pm
I, in light footsteps, was walking west along Huating Lake
When I heard frogs croaking

Ten minutes after, I saw, on my mobile phone
The photograph of the first black hole of humanity
Like the bloodshot eye of a frog
Staring at me from the centre of the Milky Way till I got home

感应

老周戴好身份牌
摸索着进电梯
这是他晚饭后的功课
公园池塘里的
鱼
在等他

可他摁了上行键
在顶层廊道里
他碰不到一个人
他只看见城市灯海里
数不清的蝌蚪
亮着，游着

在他死后几年的一晚
我在廊道遇见他
我问为什么你摁了上行键
他掏出心脏
说
你摁这个试试

Telepathy

Old Zhou, after putting on his ID card
Groped his way into the lift
This was his homework after dinner
For the fish
In the pond of the park
Were waiting for him

He pressed the button for 'Up'
But he didn't meet anyone
In the top-level corridor
All he could see, in a sea of city lights
Was countless tadpoles
Lit up, swimming

One night, years after his death
I met him in the corridor
When I asked why he pressed the button for 'Up'
He took out his heart
And said:
Please try pressing this

夜风四起

光亮的捕手
搅乱了夜

路灯下，树枝拼命挥舞
沙沙作响
如同欢迎仪式上
亢奋的孩子们

两只剥去肉瓣的橙子
静坐窗台
如果插上红烛
它们会是坚贞的
灯窟吗

The Night Wind Rose in All Directions

The catcher of lights
Disturbed the night

Under the streetlights, the tree branches were desperately waving
Rustling
Like excited kids
In a welcome ceremony

Two oranges, disembowelled
Sat still on the windowsill
If you plant the red candles in them
Will they be chaste
Lantern caves?

江湖

老爸给了一把钝刀
长满豁口和铁锈
在清水石上磨了
一整夜
"防身要紧，砍人费力
见血见肉见骨头的事
就躲远一点！"

老妈塞给我一双布鞋
鞋头还打了一层皮
"过河要当心
烘干时
离火头远一点。"

他们哪里知道
他们的儿子翻过山梁
蹚过大河
在一座陌生城堡
用刀和鞋
换了一坛老酒

醉得昏天黑地后
他光着身子唱歌
骑一头大象消失在
茂密丛林

Rivers and Lakes

Dad gave me a blunt knife
Chipped and rusty
I sharpened it on the clean-water stone
All night
'It's more important to protect yourself than to hack at people
Get further away from things
To do with blood or flesh!'

Mom gave me a pair of cloth shoes
The head of the shoes was wrapped with a skin
'Be careful when you go across a river
When you dry them
Keep away from the fire'

They didn't know
That their son had climbed over the mountains
And waded across big rivers
In a strange castle
He traded his knife and shoes
For a jar of old wine

After he got drunk, mistaking the night for the day
He sat naked, singing a song
And rode an elephant, disappearing
In a dense forest

风暴

我不会再说爱
不会再碰你
你就当我死了
一把火烧了
煮一锅开水浇了
用锋利的语言
剁碎我

吃了我
吃不完，用花椒盐腌了我
把我塞进时光空洞
弹出银河系
我不会再说爱
我恨不得现在
铰你掰你黑你白你喷你吸你

可我不会再碰你
我走
背起大理石、弹片、海滩拒马
光脚跳上电街车
绕城市一圈又一圈
直到看见，你的窗台
重新摆上星辰花

The Storm

I won't say I love you any more
I won't touch you any more
Just treat me as if I were dead
Set fire to me
Boil me in a wok
Slash me into pieces
With sharp words

Eat me up
Or, if you can't, pickle me with flowery pepper salt
Stuff me into an empty tunnel of time and space
Shoot me out of the Milky Way
I won't say I love you any more
I'd wish to
Scissor you, break you apart, blacken you, whiten you, spit you, suck you

But I won't touch you any more
I leave
Carrying granite, shrapnel, beach barricades
I'll jump barefoot onto an electric streetcar
Going around the city again and again
Till I see your windowsill
Placed with star flowers once again

悼亡灵

每天，都有灵魂逃生
在亲人酣睡的凌晨
在河流无法搅动，而星宿恰有空座
或当春天仍未洗尽冬垢
你们如风一样
穿过生命的瓶颈

想想吧，高山在大海边涌动
树叶载不动一棵树，却带走浓绿
和枯败，飞越日月的幕墙
你们像孩子，沐浴乳浆

而人间的爱总在生长
让悲伤逐渐凝结
终于长成心口的一朵灵芝

Mourning the Dead Souls

Every day, there are souls fleeing for their lives
in the wee hours when the loved ones are soundly asleep
when rivers won't stir and there are vacancies in a star
or when the spring remains uncleaned of its winter dirt
you are, like wind
going through the bottleneck of life

just have a think: tall mountains are surging by the sea
when leaves, unable to carry a tree, walk away with the dark green
and the withered, flying over the curtain wall of the sun and the moon
you are, like kids, bathing in the milk

while love keeps growing in the world
letting sorrow gradually congeal
turning into a felicitous plan, at the mouth of the heart

有一种欢聚

在大地的心脏深处，有一种欢聚
像泉水簇拥，不，像闪电灸舞
组成一个昆虫般的亲密家庭
你们鄙视饥饿与寒冷，细数回心草的根须
聆听地面亲人的足音。你们的脸
浮莲一样生动起来，幸福地疏散忧伤

A Happy Getting-Together

In the depths of the heart of the land, there is a happy getting-together
clustering, like spring water, no, like lightning, dancing a scorching dance
forming an intimate family, insect-like
you despise hunger and cold, counting the roots of the heart-returning grass
and listening to the sound of the footsteps of the loved ones. Your faces
are becoming vivid, like the floating lotuses, happily dispersing the sorrow

大山里的春色

阳光向下，春风向上
溪水在石头深处流淌
杜鹃在叫，长缓，短急
提醒一粒种子，择日破苞，着地染色
那一抹娇嫩的映山红
是大山干涸的嘴唇

我走过石桥，爬上山坡
低头走过无人的女贞树林
她们叶片圆润，枝干骨感
沙质土壤里藏着发达的须根
可是当我驻足山脊
眼睛被滚灼的山岚蒙蔽
我幽邃：大山真的想把春色囚禁？

那一声声荡气回肠的杜鹃鸣叫
在山谷中分不清是天地的本性
还是岁月的回声

Colours of the Spring in the Mountains

Sunlight downwards and spring wind upwards
the creek water was running, in the depths of the rocks
the cuckoos were cooing, long and sluggish, short and hurried
reminding a seed to break open on a chosen day, getting dyed on the ground
the azalea, tender
was the drying lips of the mountain

I was walking across the stone bridge, up the slope
and, my head lowered, past the privet trees
their leaves round and moist, their branches bone-like
their developed roots hidden in the sandy soil
but when I stopped on the mountain ridge
my eyes blinkered by the hot mountainscape
I was quietly resentful: do the mountains really want to imprison the colours
of the spring?

one couldn't tell whether the cuckoos' calls, bowl-stirring
were the nature of heaven and earth
or the echoes of the years

我索性被绿色包围

留一条青石小径
通向光影交替的幸福城堡
风水在春天的罗盘里旋转
树木花草也中了它的魔咒

谁脱去鞋帽，眼痴神迷
如同启封的酒，在轻风中摇晃
谁的心里养活许多人
谁注定成为这城堡的主人

小路边缘，有人踩着猫步
她的头发长一寸
就增添了一寸向外突围的
活力

I Simply Let Myself Be Surrounded with the Colour Green

Leave a bluestone path
connected to a happy castle of light and shadows
as wind and water are turning around in the compass
trees, flowers and grass are spellbound as well

who has shed his shoes and cap, eyes intoxicated
like uncapped liquor, swaying in the gentle breeze
whose heart keeps so many alive
and who is going to become the master of this castle

on the edge of the path, someone is walking the catwalk
the longer her hair is by one inch
the more vivacity it extends
in breaking out of its own bounds

祭酒

腊月祭祖
八仙桌兜满祭菜和祭酒
上香，焚纸，磕头
斟酒，绕桌子给每位添酒
两个时辰后收拾碗筷
一切虚拟又真实

我负责将祭酒
倒回长颈壶
拿起第 28 个小酒盅时
我的手莫名颤抖
白瓷壶落地
爆竹一样响
洒在地面的酒
很快被吸干

"那些野魂灵
有多慌渴啊！"

Libation

In the twelfth lunar month, ancestors were worshipped
the eight-deity table was laden, with sacrificial dishes and liquor
incense was offered, paper burnt, heads bowed
and liquor was served, to everyone around the table
till it was cleared two hours after
everything so virtual, and true

I was the one responsible for pouring the sacrificial liquor
back into the long-necked pot
when I picked up the 28th cup
my hand trembled, for no reason at all
when the white porcelain pot dropped
cracking like firecrackers
the liquor, spilled on the ground
quickly sucked dry

'those wild spirits
are so thirsty!'

我为什么喜欢酒

因为我觉得，越来越像你了
通过酒，你从我体内活过来
那迷醉又拘谨的笑
那迷乱又浑浊的眼神
还有那词不达意的嘴唇
让我听见，你在我体内发牢骚

你一辈子活得窝囊
和子女也很少掏心窝子
喜欢一个人，喝闷酒
喝着喝着，就长声叹息
几杯下去，才抬头看身边的亲人
这个江南水乡一样温潮的男人

这个生命最后丢失了记忆的男人
现在像酵母菌，在我的血液里流窜
并时时检举我的犬儒或流氓基因
这很好，能让我越喝越清醒
让我一次次举杯，对着脑电波中的你
示好，祝祷，弥补一个做儿子的过错

Why Do I Love Liquor?

Because I feel more and more like you
as you come alive via liquor
with your intoxicated and formal smile
your confused and turbid eye
and your inexpressible lips
which all make me hear your complaints within me

you have lived a pointless life
with hardly a heart-to-heart with your own kids
preferring to drink alone
and, as you drink, you sigh long sighs
and raise your head to look at the loved ones around you
you, someone as warm and moist as the water country in the River South

a man who lost his memory in his final years
is, like yeast, now running through my blood
and, from time to time, reports on my cynic or hooligan gene
which is good as it helps me grow more conscious the more I drink
let me hold up my cup again and again, in front of you in my brain waves
to express friendship, to pray, to make up for my mistakes as a son

三人行

98 的岳丈领着
86 大女婿，76 二女婿
约几克重的魂
走入油尽灯枯

他们
抖着帕金森的手，阿尔茨海默的
眼光，双颊塌陷

他们的肉身安置在不同床上
二女婿在养老院五楼
岳丈躺在中心医院 A 区三楼
大女婿瘫在自家的床，结婚时
铺撒过玫瑰，如今腐叶一枚
他咽气在凌晨两点到五点

忘了带走照路的光

岳丈撑到大女婿头七之后，也丢下了躯体
他要追上大女婿，以壮年身份互打招呼

二女婿是我父亲大人
当我在耳边告诉那两人的去向
他浑浊呆滞的老眼
流下三岁儿童的
眼泪

Three of Them, Walking Together

Father-in-law, at 98
led his two sons-in-law at 86 and 76
walked till the lamp withered, with dried oil
their souls weighing but a few grams

they
were trembling with Parkinson's hands, with Alzheimer's
eyes, their cheeks sunken

their bodies were situated on different beds
Son-in-law 2 on the fifth floor of the nursing home
Son-in-law 1 paralyzed in his own bed, which was strewn
with roses at the wedding, now a rotten leaf
he breathed his last between 2 a.m. and 5 a.m.

forgetting to take with him the light showing the road

Father-in-law stuck past Son-in-law 1's First Seventh Day before he died
wanting to catch up with him, greeting him like a mature man

Son-in-law 2 was my father
when I whispered to him about where the other two had gone
tears of a three-year-old
rolled out
of his old eyes, dull and turbid

祂们

看着一批批
从天上下来的人们
走出接机口
我觉得
地球人真
可爱

我还发现了天使
混在其中
祂们收起翅膀
朝我扑来

Them

Watching group after group
of people, down from the sky
coming out of the arrival hall
I thought that
the Earthlings were so
lovely

I'd also found angels
mixed amidst them
as they folded their wings
and pounced on me

谍战

我们拥有两套话语系统
一套：玫瑰、美酒、做爱和深的瞳
一套：匕首、炸弹、墓地和显影剂

两套系统并行。两人前胸贴后背
意识到，心脏正好重叠
一根铁钎可同时扎透

所以我们保持四目相对
要么看着对方死去
要么看对方身后的黑暗
崩塌

The Espionage War

We have two discourse systems
one that consists of roses, beautiful wine, lovemaking and deep pupils
and the other: daggers, bombs, graveyards and the developer

the two systems in parallel. When the two are back to back
they realize that their hearts overlap
where an iron pin can go right through

which is why we keep the four eyes in line
to either watch the other one die
or see the darkness collapse
behind the other

诗 / 大卡

油箱，备用胎，蛮横的轴承
像裸露的肌肉
车头那根排气管
管口积一层黑黑烟垢

大卡在小区掉头
低矮的树枝被撞得
咔咔响，嗤嗤的刹车声
搅得麻雀四散而逃

一个精瘦的黄毛小子
在车尾挥手跺脚
"憨卵，你会不会倒车啊！"
大卡连回几个响屁

我想起一位博士的经历
三十年前开长途大卡
某次刹车失灵，一头扎进
烟花爆竹店，几乎成就

完美庆典。他用写诗的手
在空中打着方向盘，狠狠地笑
我以为，他就是开着诗歌大卡
在狭隘腐朽的城堡左冲右突

Poetry/Truck

The fuel tank, the spare tire, and the arrogant bearing
like the exposed muscles
the exhaust pipe at the head of the truck
was cluttered with black soot at its mouth

the truck was doing a U-turn in a residential area
scraping the low branches
with a creaking noise and its braking screeches
scared the sparrows in all directions

a thin, yellow-haired young man
was stamping his feet and waving his hand at the back of the truck
'Stupid balls! Do you know how to reverse or not?'
the truck kept farting, in response

I was reminded of a doctoral guy's experience
thirty years ago, when his brake failed
driving his long-distance truck right into
a shop of firecrackers, nearly achieving

a perfect ceremony. He handled the steering wheel
with his poetry-writing hand, laughing, quite uncouthly
he was driving his poetry truck
rushing around in the narrow and decaying castle, I thought

新生物

清晨车流淙淙
那辆奥迪 Q7 左冲右突
插到我前面

一只夹烟的兰花手
伸出车窗
轻掸烟灰，又收回

在红灯区域
一股青烟从窗内喷出
片刻袅娜

我死踩油门，左闪灯
右闪灯，引擎吼叫
我要看看那张兰花脸

晨风混着庄稼气息
和汽油味，吹皱我的
鼻子，而眼神灼热

就在两车交会时
我惊愕，那辆奥迪车里
转过来一具章鱼脸

Things That Are New

Early morning. A trickle of traffic
an Audi Q7, rushing this way and that
cut in front of me

a cigarette between the orchid fingers
was extended out the window
flicking the ash off, before it was taken back

when the red lights were on
a blue smoke came spewing out the window
momentarily graceful

I, stepping on the accelerator right to the end, put on the left signal
then right, my engine roaring
as I wanted to see the orchid face

the morning wind, mixed with the crop
and the petrol, creased my
nose, and hotted up my eye

but, just when our cars met side by side
I was shocked to see that in the Audi
the face that was turned was an octopus one

湿天出行

一只蜗牛盘吸在车门
潮湿的气流里
好像听见它在哼唧

一枚白蝴蝶从顶棚飞出
贴一会儿挡风玻璃
又落到后座上

我带它们一路东行
或许还可带一尾、一羽、一匹
一头什么的向一座岛冲去

就在长江的入海口
这么多一，被海风泡大
而那些胖云拧得出水来

好吧。现在让蝴蝶驮起蜗牛
蜗牛驮起我
我驮起这座岛吧

Going Out on a Wet Day

A snail was sucking on the car door
and one could hear its mumbling
in the moist air-current

a white butterfly flew from underneath the roof
and got stuck on the windshield
before it dropped in the backseat

I went all the way east, with them
and I could possibly take a tail, a feather, a head
or a bolt of something, rushing towards an island

right at the estuary of the Yangtze
there were so many ones, soaked by the wind, until big
and water could be squeezed out of those fat clouds

all right. Let the butterfly carry the snail on its back
let the snail carry me on its back
and let me carry this island on my back then

演化

一声鸟鸣和另一声鸟鸣
叠加成林子

一条游鱼和另一条游鱼
汇聚成海子

一座青峰和另一座青峰
连绵成山脉

一个人和另一个人
一簇烟火和另一簇烟火

一抔骨灰和另一抔骨灰
合眠在同一个坟冢

一枚蝴蝶和另一枚蝴蝶
化成悲喜符号

Evolution

A birdcall and another birdcall
overlapped into a wood

a swimming fish and another swimming fish
converged into a sea

a green peak and another green peak
meandered in a mountain ridge

a person and another person
a cluster of fire and another cluster of fire

a handful of bone-ashes and another handful of bone-ashes
sleep together in one grave

a butterfly and another butterfly
turn into a symbol of happy sorrow

水樱桃

我盯着水中
六枚樱桃
大的沉底
小的半浮
她们不同侧面
泛着紫光
青褐色果蒂
搭在彼此身上

有一枚
饱满表皮
冒出了几个水泡
是长时间的凝视
让她有了呼吸

Water Cherries

I was staring at the six
cherries in the water
the big ones had sunk to the bottom
and the small ones were half floating
their different sides
shone purple
the green and brown stems
on top of each other

one cherry
full-skinned
spat a few bubbles
it was my long stare
that gave her breathing

催眠

一只鹰，站在崖顶
观测初夏的风
从谷底升腾

清凉来自溪涧
来自难以想象的满山坡
大滨菊、玉蝉花和桔梗

来自大地广博而质朴的幸福感
像母亲，又像孩子
等待一种雄性，君临

或催眠。长空一声鹰唳
牠张开翅膀，用阴影
收割每一个慵躺的意志

Hypnosis

An eagle, standing on top of the cliff
was observing the early summer wind
arising from the bottom of the valley

coolness came from the creeks
the incredible chrysanthemums, irises and balloon flowers
that were covering all the mountain slope

and from the happiness, vast and simple, of the land
like mother, like children
waiting for a male, to descend

or to render hypnotic. With a cry in the long sky, the eagle
opened its wings and harvested every lazy will
with its shadow

易拉罐

课堂上给学生
观看美国影片《奇迹男孩》
看到被忽略、被损害、被霸凌
的少男少女最终
拥有追光灯与掌声时
我看到很多学生
在抹眼睛

坐在前排的姚远
一边抹眼睛
一边使劲捏空易拉罐
"嘎啦嘎啦"的金属声
撕扯大家的耳膜
我知道，他在努力抵抗
碳酸情绪

我以手做枪
向他点射
他向后一仰
易拉罐骨碌碌地响

Pop-Up Cans

In class, I got my students to watch
Wonder, an American film
and saw many of them
wipe the tears from their eyes
when they saw how the ignored, hurt and bullied
teenagers end up
having the spotlight and applause

Yao Yuan, sitting in the front row
was wiping the tears
as he pulled open a pop-up can
the cracking metal noise
grating on the ear
I knew that he was resisting
the carbonic acid mood

with my hand in the shape of a pistol
I shot at him
when he tipped backwards
his can gurgling

尖叫

她在楼道里嚷嚷
用尖尖的假嗓
好像在和谁理论
也不知道争什么，只是尖尖地
高低不定地对
空气撒气

她又跑到楼外空地
继续尖叫
渐渐有一种荡秋千的腔调
我知道她很享受
蚕豆眼冲天辫
爱理不理

我猜测午休的园长脸都拧成
波斯菊啦
想想，心里有些痛快
我也想跑出去对着阳光叫
我嗓子里也有条毛毛虫
可是她忽然不叫了

静得可怕

Screaming

She was screaming
in falsetto
in the corridor
as if she was arguing with someone
but no one knew what it was about except that it's a sharp voice
getting angry with the air
in tones high and low

once again she ran out to the open ground outside the building
and kept on screaming
now sounding like on a swing
I knew she was enjoying herself
her broad-bean eyes and her sky-high pigtail
giving you the go-bye

I guessed that the face of the kindergarten manager, having a siesta then
must have turned into a garden cosmos
the more I thought of it the happier I became
so much so that I wanted to run out and yell at the sunlight
as there was also a caterpillar in my throat
but, all of a sudden, she stopped screaming

when everything became terrifyingly quiet

疑似抑郁症

我天生皮肤很白
上面浮一层虚火
我总是低眼看人
白眼球泛些蛋青色
我的笑有一种铁皮
被用力撕开的感觉

妈妈，我抑郁啦
今天我可以不用上学吗？

妈妈停止咬指甲
把一盆仙人掌丢进
抽水马桶
她喜欢听马桶抽水的声音
她说，我不管
这次你数学考不过 80
我就和你爸离婚

所以老师请你原谅我
试卷的 22 分我改成了
88。我不想他们离婚
我喜欢做他们的抑郁女儿

It Seems That I'm Depressed

I was born white-skinned
with a pale fire floating on my skin
I always look down on people
the white of my eye glimmering with egg blue
and my smile felt like an iron skin
forcibly torn open

Mom, I'm depressed
Can I skip school today?

Mom stopped biting her nails
to chuck a pot of cactus
into the flush toilet
as she liked listening to its noise
she said: I don't care
If you don't pass the maths exam this time round
I'll divorce your Dad

So, please, Teacher, can you forgive me
as I have changed the marks on the exam from 22 to 88
because I didn't want them to divorce
and I want to be their depressed daughter

跑题

身为"归正人"的辛弃疾
因受歧视而不被重用
真是个憋屈啊
但他大半生和女真族杠上了
终了还是"唤取红巾翠袖，
揾英雄泪！"

请问在座的谁不是汉族
朱怡菁慢慢举手，说老师
我是壮族
曾因轻度抑郁症休养在家
她的肤色苍白中泛些蛋青
在汉族群体里举起了手

我的耳边响起了
刘三姐的歌声

A Digression

Xin Qiji, as a returnee to Orthodoxy
was not prized as he was discriminated against
it's so awful
but he had spent more than half of his life against the Jurchen people
and, in the end, had to wonder who was there, among the singing girls
to wipe the tears of a hero

'Can I ask who is not of the Han ethnicity in this class please?'
Zhu Yijing held up her hand slowly and said, 'Teacher
I'm of the Zhuang ethnicity
I rested at home for a while because I was suffering from slight depression'
her pale skin was shimmering with egg blue
and she was holding up her hand among the Han-Chinese group

a song, 'Third Sister Liu', started ringing
in my ears

美少女日记

腊月二十五，阳光挺好
可以洗羊毛衫
隔壁王大哥明天回老家
整了一大桌子菜
他老婆扭着肥腰洗头
总是用剜肉的眼神
看我

房东的儿女
回来祭祖
上灯后那暖锅嘟嘟嘟响
笑着，说冒泡的话
咕嘟咕嘟冒泡的话
难得静一会儿
很快又咕嘟咕嘟地响

房东女婿喝多了
总是用剜肉的眼神看我
我的臀紧紧的
腰细细的，都说我像田小娥
离开的时候我就趴窗
等他走过窗子
我狠狠电他

Diary Entry, by a Beautiful Girl

25th, in the twelfth month of the lunar year, the sun is good
I can wash my woolen jumper
Because Big Brother Wang next door is going back to his hometown tomorrow
He has prepared a full table of dishes
His wife is washing her hair, twisting her fat waist
She always looks at me
Cuttingly

The son and daughter of my landlord
Have come back to pay respects to their ancestors
When the lamp is lit, the hot pot is tooting
They laugh and chat, with bubbling words
Gurgling, bubbling words
They hardly become quiet
Before they make gurgling noise again

When the son-in-law of my landlord drinks a lot
He looks at me, cuttingly
My hips are tight
My waist thin. They all say I look like Tian Xiao'e
When they leave I'll lean against the window
And I'll electrocute him
When he goes past the window

海拉尔

在海边就已说好
你写《碰咚》塞进海嘴
海有多无聊
干脆把碰咚塞进海嘴
你扣上救生衣
从小船驳上大船
在醉酒般的晃荡中写好了
《碰咚》：我不管了啊
海，张开你的大嘴巴
我要拉了。来了，听……

拉完《碰咚》你一脸爽透
指着我鼻子说，快
赶紧写，岸上就说好的
我涎着脸说，不行啊
我怕海嘴咬我的屁蛋蛋
还是回岸上再说吧

在岸上我说写《海拉尔》
我说你读读这三个字：
海——拉——尔——
口型、气息、舌位、颚颤
全有了，比你的《碰咚》
洋气得海了去了
直到现在我写出上面这些
仍在嗫瑟地朗读：
海——拉——尔——

Hai—La—Erh

We agreed by the seaside
that you'd write 'Plop' and shove it into the sea mouth
as the sea was so boring
you'd better shove it right into the sea mouth
you buttoned up the life jacket
boarded the big ship from the small
and finished writing 'Plop'
on the strength of the drunken swaying:
I wouldn't give a damn
Sea, open your mouth wide
I'll push, coming. Listen...

when you finished pushing with 'Plop', you looked so comforted
pointing to my nose and said: Quick
Write yours down as we agreed on shore
Brazen-faced, I said: No, I can't
I'm afraid of the sea mouth biting off my balls
Let's talk about it when we get ashore

Back on shore I said I'd write 'Hai—La—Erh'
I said just you read these three characters aloud:
Hai—La—Erh—
The shape of the mouth, the breath, the position of the tongue, and the tremor
of the jaws
Everything is there, much more oceanic
Than your 'Plop'
Even now when I have put down the above
I still am proud enough to read them out loud:
Hai—La—Erh—

数数

1, 2, 3, 4
你数吧
5, 6, 7, 8
你再数
9, 10, 11, 12

你还数吗，你不数了
好吧，我数

12, 11, 10, 9
你还记得
8, 7, 6, 5

你说，还数吗
这样数下去有意思吗

4, 3, 2, 1
好了，不数了
来吧，亲爱的，来吧
再把你的脚趾给我
我来唇数

Counting the Numbers

1, 2, 3 and 4
You count
5, 6, 7 and 8
You keep counting
9, 10, 11 and 12

Will you still count? No?
Alright, I'll count

12, 11, 10 and 9
You still remember
8, 7, 6 and 5?

You say: Still want to count?
Any point keeping counting on?

4, 3, 2 and 1
Alright, no more
Come on, my dear, come on
Show me your toes again
And let me lip-count them

"闯虎穴"

看守所秦所是我哥们
他的左手边依次是

OK 厅妈咪
　（现在是这家店的老板娘）
学车教练孙二娘
　（她老公刚被判了刑）
包租婆扈三娘
　（大胸脯上吊了颗祖母绿）
迟到了 10 分钟的孙红英
　（不停打电话催她的麻友）

最后是财气大粗的朱老板
　（右手残掌，仅剩拇指和小指
喝酒时，二指禅一点不含糊）
鄙人，一位教师和诗人
　（这些我没让秦所介绍）
敬酒嗓门粗了，碰杯话语野了
真把自己当成威虎山的杨子荣

我一直记得和朱老板握手
就像钳住了生活的蟹螯

'Storming into a Tiger's Den'

Director Qin, of a detention station, was my bro
on his left-hand side, and in sequential order was

Madam of a Kala-OK Night Club
(right now, its boss)
Sun Erniang, a driving instructor
(her husband has just been jailed)
Hu Sanniang, a landlady
(an emerald hanging down her big breasts)
Sun Hongying who was 10 minutes late
(and kept calling her Mahjong friend to hurry up)

at the end was Boss Zhu, a tycoon
(whose right hand has only a thumb and a little finger
but when he drinks, his two-finger zen could work wonders)
and I myself, a teacher and a poet
(I didn't let Director Qin tell them *that*)
I toasted them till my throat turned thick and my words became wild
actually treating myself as Yang Zirong in *The Taking of the Tiger Mountain*

I still remember that when I shook hands with Boss Zhu
it felt like shaking the claws of a crab

好的，瑞雪

我说瑞雪，你有空来一下
瑞雪的头像很快闪，说好的

其间真的下雪了，越下越大
雪花落在狗身上，被甩成一团雾

落在树枝上，变得毛茸茸
落在水塘里，瞬间有凄美

直到夜色降临，灯光下的雪
像血液燃烧的情人，撒野……

翌日，雪后初霁。我问瑞雪
你昨天答应了，为何又没来

瑞雪的头像很快闪闪，说是呀
你说有空来，凭我一昨天没空啊

Alright, Auspicious Snow

I said: Auspicious Snow. Come here when you got a minute
Auspicious Snow flashed its head and said: Okay then

The snow really fell, becoming bigger and bigger
When snowflakes fell on a dog, it was whipped into a fog

When they fell on the branches, they turned hairy
And when they fell into a pond, there was an instant beauty

It's not till nightfall when the snow in the lights
Went wild, like lovers whose blood was burning...

The next day when the snow stopped I asked Ruixue (Auspicious Snow)
You promised to come yesterday but why are you not coming?

Ruixue flashed its head and said: Right
You said to come when I got a minute. But I got no time all day yesterday

求救腔

车下德清服务站
一窝人蜂拥而入洗手间
那位来自澳大利亚的
　　黄冈籍诗人
甩开臂膀挤入
　　这膀胱大合唱

听：嘘嘘的，弋阳腔
　　　嗤嗤的，松江腔
　　　铿铿的，瀛洲腔
　　　滤滤的，悉尼腔
　　　嗖嗖的，乌鲁木齐腔
　　　噔噔的，营口盘锦张掖腔

写出《阿旺尕》笑翻全场的
澳籍黄冈湖滨楼诗人
甩着膀子钻出另一个出口
他找不到原来的车子
手机呼叫："玩死你，赶紧来救我
我在长三角公安检测口！"

Sounding the Alarm

When our van arrived at Deqing Service Station
we all went out, streaming into the toilet
the Australian poet
    originally from Huanggang
his arms swinging
    joined the chorus of bladders

Listen:
    Shoo shoo, the accent of Yiyang
    Chih chih, that of Songjiang
    Ken ken, that of Yingzhou
    Loo loo, that of Sydney
    Soo soo, that of Urumqi
    Deng deng, that of Yingkou, Panjin and Zhangye

the poet from Lake Hotel, Huanggang and Australia
who brought the house down with his 'Ah Wang Gah'
his arms swinging, crept out from another exit
unable to find the van
he called out on his mobile phone: 'I'll play you dead! Come and rescue me. Quick
I am at the Yangtze River Delta Public Security Inspection Depot!'

心脏搭桥者言

泥石流、堰塞湖、山体崩塌
硬化、风化、点卤水
地震、海啸、强台风
违章、拆迁、非法上访
交通堵塞、下水道堵塞、网络瘫痪
经济制裁、定时炸弹、萨德系统、巴别塔
教堂、火车站、太平间和健忘村的
时钟蒙尘，锈蚀，发条绵软成油条
············
在我们体内
时时发生

Thus Spoke the One Having Gone Through the Heart Bypass

Mudslides, avalanche lakes, landslides

Hardening, weather-exposed and getting soaked in brine

Earthquakes, tsunamis and strong typhoons

Violating the rules, demolitions and illegal petitions

Traffic jams, sewer blockages and internet paralysis

Economic sanctions, time bombs, THAAD, and Babel Tower

Churches, train stations, morgues and the dust-covered clocks

In the Village of Forgetfulness, getting rusty, with the clockwork softened, like *youtiao*

…

Things that frequently happen

Inside us

江小白

"嗯，一份拍黄瓜
一碟花生米，一盆酸菜鱼
再加两瓶江小白。"
"好的。就一个人吗？"
"你们的江小白几两一个？"
"二两、半斤都有。您一个人吗？"
"那就来两个二两的江小白。"
"好的，你一个人的话，请里面坐。"
"姑娘，为什么一个人就坐里面呢？"
"里面安静。等会儿歌厅散场，
他们一伙伙来宵夜的。"
··········
"姑娘，这江小白不会是假的吧？"
"不会哟，江小白很正宗滴~~。"
"你没喝咋知道正宗滴~~？"
"大哥，我就是重庆滴，江小白
重庆很有名的噻。"
··········
"小妹，再来一瓶江小白！"
"好，大哥稍等，我先给她们上菜。"
"我是江小白，生活很简单。
广告上这么说的。
不要到处宣扬你的内心，
因为不止你一人有故事。
广告上还这么说。"
··········
"大哥，你为啥子喜欢江小白？"
"大哥肯定看过《北上广依然相信爱情》，

River Little White (Or Jiang Xiao Bai)

'Oomph, one smashed cucumber salad

a dish of peanuts, a basin of sour vegetable fish

and two bottles of Jiang Xiao Bai'

'Sure. Only one person?'

'What's the size of one bottle?'

'It varies from 100g to 250g. Just you alone?'

'Then bring me two bottles of 100g'

'Okay. If you are alone, please sit inside'

'Girl, why should I sit inside if I'm alone?'

'It's quiet inside. In a little while when the Song and Dance Hall closes

they'll come here in groups for a late meal'

…

'Girl, the Jiang Xiao Bai is not fake?'

'No way. It has got to be authentic~~'

'If you don't drink, how do you know it's authentic~~?'

'Big Brother, I'm from Chongqing and Jiang Xiao Bai

is well-known in Chongqing'

…

'Little Sister, bring me another Jiang Xiao Bai!'

'Okay, Big Brother. Just a minute as I'm serving them.'

'I am Jiang Xiao Bai. Life is simple

That's what is said on the advertisement

Don't advertise your heart of hearts

Because you are not the only one to have a story to tell'

…

'Big Brother, why do you like Jiang Xiao Bai'

'Big Brother, you must have watched *City Still Believes in Love*,

里面的王茂哥好嗑这一口。"

"姑娘，你咋知道哥就叫王茂呢？"

⋯⋯⋯⋯⋯

"哥，你喝多啦，能回去吗？"

"不行，你去叫江小白过来，
陪哥继续喝⋯⋯"

⋯⋯⋯⋯⋯

"王茂哥，江小白全在你肚子里啦！"

"黄依然，这里真的是⋯⋯重庆吗？"

Brother Wang Mao in it just loves drinking it'

'Girl, how do you know I am Brother Wang Mao?'

...

'Brother, you've had a bit too much. Can you find your way home?'

'No. You go and get Jiang Xiao Bai to come

To keep me company and drink more...'

...

'Brother Wang Mao, Jiang Xiao Bai is now in your belly!'

'Huang Yiran, is this really Chongqing here?'

金色烟蒂

一大片草地
起伏
树荫底下
我们抽烟
聊天
说：置之死地而后生
说：声誉鹊起即
危机四伏

而我们等的那个人
还未出现在
那座桥上
他远道而来
身怀利器
但是经常在林中迷路

我们在树荫底下等
在一大片
起伏的草地上
发现了
一枚金色烟蒂
像子弹壳

A Golden Butt

A spread of heaving
grassland
in the shade of a tree
we were smoking
and chatting
one said: Coming alive in death
one said: Fame is followed
by crisis after crisis

and the person we were waiting for
had not appeared
on the bridge
he had come from afar
carrying something sharp
but he had often got lost in the woods

we were waiting in the tree shade
on a vast spread of grassland
we discovered
a golden cigarette butt
like a bullet shell

暴雨核心

其实已经知道这场暴雨
必然到来：天空铅硬
乌云堆积成熊黑虎豹
空气中散发着硫磺味

白桦树站在原地不动
等待，还有点兴奋
毫无理由地被推进
这场暴雨的核心

其实除了雨珠很疯狂
甚至有点歇斯底里
乌云也没那么狰狞
站在核心的也可能不是

白桦树，只是因为形象气质
还有惯常的欣赏需求
如果需要，它也可以劈成柴
那就成了火焰的核心

The Centre of the Storm

In fact, I already knew that this storm
was definitely coming: the sky lead-hard
dark clouds heaped up, like tigers, lions and bears
the air was sulfurous

the birch tree stood still where it was
waiting, slightly excited
thrust into the centre of this storm
without a reason

in fact, except that the raindrops were crazy
a little hysterical
the dark clouds were not so ferocious
and the one standing in the centre might not be

the birch tree; it was there because of its image
and the habitual need for aesthetics
if need be, it could be cut into firewood
that turned into the centre of flames